# MAKING MONEY ONLINE: BOOK 5

## BY MICHAEL CALLUM MAYAKA

# ONLINE TUTORING AND EDUCATION

# FOREWORD:

In today's digital age, making money online has become a viable and accessible option for individuals seeking financial independence or additional income streams. The internet offers a plethora of opportunities that allow you to leverage your skills, creativity, and resources to generate revenue. This guide aims to provide you with valuable insights, strategies, and practical tips on how to make money online effectively.

This book is part of a series for more information see Further reading at the end of this book.

# Table of Contents

Foreword: ........................................................................................... 3

5. Online Tutoring and Education .................................................. 5

   5.1 Virtual Tutoring Platforms .................................................. 6

      Benefits of Virtual Tutoring Platforms: ............................. 7

      Getting Involved in Virtual Tutoring Platforms: ........... 10

      Conclusion: ......................................................................... 13

   5.2 Creating Online Courses and Educational Content ........ 15

      1. Identify your expertise and target audience: ............... 16

      2. Define learning objectives and structure: ................... 17

      3. Create high-quality content: ......................................... 18

      4. Choose the right platform: ............................................ 18

      5. Engage and interact with your learners: ..................... 20

      6. Market and promote your course: ............................... 20

      7. Gather feedback and make improvements: ................ 21

      8. Stay updated and expand your offerings: ................... 22

   5.3 Language Instruction and Translation Services: Unlocking the Power of Communication .................................................... 24

      1. Language Instruction: .................................................... 25

      2. Translation Services: ...................................................... 28

Further reading: ............................................................................. 33

# 5. ONLINE TUTORING AND EDUCATION

## 5.1 VIRTUAL TUTORING PLATFORMS

Virtual tutoring has emerged as a popular and effective way to share knowledge and provide educational assistance to learners around the world. With the advent of technology and internet connectivity, virtual tutoring platforms have become a convenient and accessible option for both tutors and students. This section will explore the concept of virtual tutoring platforms, their benefits, and how you can get involved.

Virtual tutoring platforms are online platforms that connect tutors with students seeking academic support or skill development. These platforms serve as intermediaries, facilitating the matching process and providing a virtual environment for tutoring sessions. They offer a range of subjects and disciplines, catering to various academic levels, including K-12, college-level courses, and specialized skills.

## BENEFITS OF VIRTUAL TUTORING PLATFORMS:

1. Accessibility: Virtual tutoring platforms break geographical barriers, allowing students to connect with qualified tutors from anywhere in the world. Students can access expert guidance and resources regardless of their location, ensuring equal educational opportunities.

2. Convenience: Online tutoring eliminates the need for physical travel, saving time and effort for both tutors and students. Sessions can be scheduled flexibly, accommodating diverse time zones and personal commitments. Students can learn from the comfort of their own homes, fostering a relaxed and focused learning environment.

3. Personalization: Virtual tutoring platforms often offer personalized learning experiences. Tutors can tailor their teaching approaches to meet individual student needs, addressing specific challenges and adapting the curriculum accordingly. This

personalized attention enhances learning outcomes and student engagement.

4. Variety of Subjects: These platforms typically provide a wide range of subjects and disciplines, covering academic subjects such as math, science, languages, and humanities, as well as specialized skills like music, coding, and test preparation. Students can find tutors who specialize in their desired areas of study.

## GETTING INVOLVED IN VIRTUAL TUTORING PLATFORMS:

1. Research and Choose a Platform: Start by exploring different virtual tutoring platforms available online. Look for platforms that align with your subject expertise, teaching style, and desired student age range. Research their reputation, user reviews, and policies to ensure credibility and professionalism.

2. Create a Profile: Once you select a platform, create a profile that highlights your qualifications, teaching experience, and any specialized skills you offer. Include relevant certifications, degrees, and

achievements to build credibility and attract potential students.

3. Set Competitive Pricing: Determine your tutoring rates based on factors such as your qualifications, experience, subject demand, and market trends. Consider starting with competitive pricing to attract your initial student base. As you gain experience and positive reviews, you can adjust your rates accordingly.

4. Develop Engaging Content: Create engaging teaching materials and resources that align with the curriculum and student goals. Prepare lesson plans, worksheets, and interactive activities to enhance the learning

experience. Incorporate multimedia elements, such as videos or presentations, to make your sessions more dynamic and effective.

5. Market Your Services: Promote your tutoring services through various channels, including social media platforms, educational forums, and online communities. Utilize the platform's marketing tools, such as featured listings or profile enhancements, to increase visibility and attract potential students.

6. Provide Excellent Service: Deliver high-quality tutoring sessions that focus on student progress and learning outcomes. Be

punctual, organized, and responsive to student inquiries. Establish a positive rapport with your students, fostering a supportive and motivating learning environment.

## CONCLUSION:

Virtual tutoring platforms have revolutionized the way educational support is delivered. They offer convenience, accessibility, and personalized learning experiences for both tutors and students. By researching and selecting the right platform, creating an engaging profile, and delivering excellent tutoring services, you can leverage virtual tutoring platforms to share your knowledge, make a positive impact on students' lives, and generate income from the comfort of your own home.

## 5.2 CREATING ONLINE COURSES AND EDUCATIONAL CONTENT

In recent years, the demand for online learning has skyrocketed, making it an excellent opportunity for individuals to create and sell online courses and educational content. Whether you're an expert in a specific field or have a passion for teaching, online education allows you to share your knowledge and expertise with a global audience. In this section, we'll explore the process of creating online courses and educational content, along with tips to make them successful.

## 1. IDENTIFY YOUR EXPERTISE AND TARGET AUDIENCE:

Before diving into course creation, identify your areas of expertise and the specific audience you want to target. Consider your knowledge, skills, and experiences that make you qualified to teach a particular subject. Defining your target audience will help tailor your content and marketing efforts to attract the right learners.

## 2. DEFINE LEARNING OBJECTIVES AND STRUCTURE:

Outline the learning objectives and outcomes you want your students to achieve through your course. This will guide you in structuring your content effectively. Break down the course into modules or lessons, ensuring a logical flow of information. Use a mix of text, images, videos, quizzes, and assignments to engage your learners and promote active participation.

## 3. CREATE HIGH-QUALITY CONTENT:

Invest time and effort in creating high-quality content that adds value to your students' learning experience. Organize your content in a structured and easily digestible format. Use clear and concise language, visuals, and multimedia elements to enhance comprehension. Incorporate real-life examples and case studies to make the content more relatable and practical.

## 4. CHOOSE THE RIGHT PLATFORM:

Selecting the right platform to host and deliver your online course is crucial. There are numerous learning management systems (LMS) available, such as Udemy, Teachable, and Coursera. Research and compare the features, pricing, and audience reach of different platforms to find the one that aligns with your goals and target audience.

## 5. ENGAGE AND INTERACT WITH YOUR LEARNERS:

Encourage active participation and engagement by incorporating interactive elements into your course. Include quizzes, discussions, and assignments to promote learner interaction. Respond promptly to student inquiries and provide constructive feedback on assignments and assessments. Consider hosting live webinars or Q&A sessions to foster a sense of community and enhance the learning experience.

## 6. MARKET AND PROMOTE YOUR COURSE:

Creating a great course is only part of the equation; you also need to effectively

By creating online courses and educational content, you have the opportunity to share your knowledge, empower learners, and generate income. Remember to focus on quality, engage with your learners, market your courses effectively, and continuously improve your offerings. With dedication and the right approach, your online courses can become a valuable asset in the world of online education.

## 5.3 LANGUAGE INSTRUCTION AND TRANSLATION SERVICES: UNLOCKING THE POWER OF COMMUNICATION

In today's interconnected world, language instruction and translation services play a vital role in bridging gaps and fostering effective communication across cultures. Whether you are passionate about teaching languages or possess strong linguistic skills, these online opportunities can provide a fulfilling and lucrative path to making money online. This section will explore the realm of language instruction and translation services, highlighting the possibilities and strategies to succeed in this field.

and Coursera. Research and compare the features, pricing, and audience reach of different platforms to find the one that aligns with your goals and target audience.

## 5. ENGAGE AND INTERACT WITH YOUR LEARNERS:

Encourage active participation and engagement by incorporating interactive elements into your course. Include quizzes, discussions, and assignments to promote learner interaction. Respond promptly to student inquiries and provide constructive feedback on assignments and assessments. Consider hosting live webinars or Q&A sessions to foster a sense of community and enhance the learning experience.

## 6. MARKET AND PROMOTE YOUR COURSE:

Creating a great course is only part of the equation; you also need to effectively market and promote it. Develop a marketing strategy that includes creating compelling course descriptions, utilizing social media platforms, collaborating with influencers or relevant websites, and offering limited-time promotions or discounts. Leverage email marketing to build an email list and communicate with potential learners regularly.

## 7. GATHER FEEDBACK AND MAKE IMPROVEMENTS:

Continuously seek feedback from your students to improve the quality of your course. Encourage learners to provide reviews and testimonials, which can significantly impact your course's reputation and visibility. Analyze feedback and make necessary updates or additions to enhance the learning experience and address any gaps.

## 8. STAY UPDATED AND EXPAND YOUR OFFERINGS:

Education is an ever-evolving field, so it's essential to stay updated with the latest trends and advancements in your subject area. Consider expanding your offerings by creating additional courses or updating existing ones to cater to changing learner needs. Keep an eye on emerging technologies, instructional methods, and industry developments to provide relevant and up-to-date content.

## 1. LANGUAGE INSTRUCTION:

Language instruction has witnessed a significant shift from traditional classroom settings to online platforms, offering flexible learning options for students and lucrative opportunities for language instructors. Online language instruction allows individuals with fluency in a particular language to share their knowledge and teach learners from around the world. Here are some key aspects to consider:

a. Identify your language expertise: Determine the language(s) you are proficient in and passionate about teaching. This could include popular languages like

English, Spanish, Mandarin, or niche languages with high demand.

b. Choose the right platform: Research and select reputable online language learning platforms that connect teachers with students. Popular platforms include iTalki, Verbling, Preply, and VIPKid.

c. Build your profile: Create an engaging profile that highlights your qualifications, teaching experience, and teaching style. Offer trial lessons or discounted rates to attract initial students and build your reputation.

d. Develop teaching materials: Prepare comprehensive lesson plans, exercises, and learning resources to facilitate effective language instruction. Consider incorporating multimedia elements, interactive activities, and gamification to enhance the learning experience.

e. Promote your services: Utilize social media platforms, online communities, and language learning forums to market your services. Encourage satisfied students to provide testimonials and recommendations.

f. Continual professional development: Stay updated with the latest teaching methodologies, language trends, and cultural nuances to deliver high-quality instruction. Join teacher communities and attend webinars or workshops to enhance your teaching skills.

## 2. TRANSLATION SERVICES:

As businesses and individuals seek to expand their global reach, the demand for professional translation services has soared. If you possess strong language skills and a keen eye for detail, offering translation services can be a profitable online venture. Consider the following steps:

a. Determine your language pairs: Identify the languages you are proficient in and the language pairs you can offer translation services for. Common language pairs include English-Spanish, English-French, or Japanese-English.

b. Specialize in specific domains: Consider specializing in a particular field, such as legal, medical, technical, or marketing translations. This allows you to develop expertise in specific terminology and attract clients from those industries.

c. Create a professional portfolio: Compile samples of your translation work to showcase your skills and capabilities. Highlight your experience, qualifications, and any certifications you possess.

d. Establish your rates: Research industry standards and set competitive rates for your translation services. Consider factors such as complexity, word count, and urgency when determining your pricing structure.

e. Network and market your services: Join professional translation associations, online freelancer platforms like Upwork or Freelancer, and reach out to potential clients directly. Utilize online marketing techniques, such as SEO optimization and content creation, to increase your visibility.

f. Invest in translation tools: Familiarize yourself with translation software, CAT tools (computer-assisted translation), and terminology management systems to improve efficiency and accuracy. These tools can streamline your workflow and enhance productivity.

Remember, in both language instruction and translation services, maintaining professionalism, meeting deadlines, and delivering high-quality work are crucial for building a strong reputation and attracting a steady stream of clients. Continually honing your language skills, staying abreast of industry trends, and seeking feedback from clients will enable you to thrive in this competitive online arena. By helping individuals communicate effectively or bridging language barriers for businesses, you can find fulfilment and financial success in language instruction and translation services.

# FURTHER READING:

If you enjoyed this book, please consider reading one of the other books in the series:

Making Money Online: Book 1 (Understanding the Online Landscape)

Making Money Online: Book 2 (E-commerce and Online Retail)

Making Money Online: Book 3 (Freelancing and Remote Work)

Making Money Online: Book 4 (Content Creation and Monetization)

Making Money Online: Book 5 (Online Tutoring and Education)

Making Money Online: Book 6 (Online Surveys, Microtasks, and Rewards)

Making Money Online: Book 7 (Online Investments and Trading)

Making Money Online: Book 8 (Creating and Selling Digital Assets)

Making Money Online: Book 9 (Online Consulting and Coaching)

Making Money Online: Book 10 (Maximizing Online Income Opportunities)

All the books can be found on Amazon as Kindle and Paperback, or you can buy the complete edition which contains the full series in one book. The complete edition is available as Kindle, Paperback and exclusively as Hardback. You can find all the links in my book site: books.michaelmayaka.co.uk.

www.ingramcontent.com/pod-product-compliance
Lightning Source LLC
Chambersburg PA
CBHW040259220526
45473CB00002B/536